Prayers for Dark People

A CREED

A LITANY

AND

DIVERS PRAYERS

SET DOWN FOR

THE WORSHIP OF

THE DARKER

AMERICANS

W. E. B. DU BOIS

Prayers for Dark People

Edited by Herbert Aptheker

THE UNIVERSITY OF MASSACHUSETTS PRESS
AMHERST

Copyright © 1980 by
The University of Massachusetts Press
All rights reserved
LC 80–12234
ISBN 0–87023–303–3 (paper)
Printed in the United States of America
Library of Congress Cataloging in Publication Data
appear on the last printed page of this book.

Introduction

Among the letters and papers entrusted into my care by Dr. Du Bois in 1961, shortly before his departure for Ghana, is an aged brown manila envelope such as one uses to mail booklets. Printed in its left-hand corner is a request to the postmaster to return the envelope to Atlanta University in Georgia, "should this pamphlet miscarry or remain uncalled for 10 days."

On the face of the envelope an addressee's name had been crossed out and above it, and again to its right, is the word, "Prayers," in Du Bois's handwriting. Below this, also in his hand and in pencil, is his signature. Within are scraps of paper of varying sizes; on each scrap Du Bois wrote a prayer—most are in pencil, a few in ink. Ten, numbered by him in pencil, are typed; these appear toward the close of this book, retaining the numbers as in the originals. In most cases, the Biblical source or inspiration is noted by Du Bois at the conclusion of his text; these are retained.

The titles as given here were written in pencil on a separate sheet, again in his own hand. In the envelope, he wrote in pencil a list of subjects; a few were treated or touched upon in the prayers that followed but most were not. This list is reproduced here, following the title page.

The date of this manuscript as a whole may be placed, with considerable confidence, as extending from early 1909 until the spring of 1910. The second prayer, devoted to "the curse of drunkenness," refers to a poet afflicted with this "curse" who had been born "100 years ago this night"; Edgar Allan Poe was born January 19, 1809. Another of the prayers, found on page 19 —as stated in a footnote—bore on its reverse side a notation, in Du Bois's handwriting, "May 3, 1910." Since

Du Bois left Atlanta University for New York City, to take up his duties with the just-founded National Association for the Advancement of Colored People, in mid-June 1910, this date would mark the latest limits for these prayers.

When I first opened this envelope the slips of paper were without any order—simply inserted helter-skelter. From the content of the prayers, up to the one dated May 3, 1910, I have deduced the probable month of delivery. In the closing section of this book the prayers are published according to the numbers Du Bois gave them; the concluding sermon, called "Cleanliness" by Du Bois, seems to belong with the numbered ones and has been placed at the end.

In one case (on page 44) Du Bois's manuscript was a fragment breaking off in the middle of a sentence; it is printed as he wrote it. In another case (on page 48) the original manuscript contains two versions of a single effort; the differences are substantial enough so that both versions are printed.

The manuscripts are published precisely as in the original, except that ampersands appear as *and*, deletions made by Du Bois are not indicated, and obvious errors in spelling are silently corrected. The title "Promptness," on page 72 has been added by the editor, as the brackets indicate.

The old Atlanta University is not to be confused with the present Atlanta University Center. The latter was organized in 1929 when the original Atlanta University, chartered in 1867, together with Morehouse College, founded the same year, and Spelman College (for Women), founded in 1881, joined to create the Center. Under that arrangement, Atlanta University was thereafter to be the graduate training division of the Center.

When Du Bois joined Atlanta University in 1897 as a professor of economics and sociology it was an institution which contained a primary school, grammar school, high school and college.* He remained in this institution until Commencement of 1910, and it is for the youngsters at this university that he wrote these prayers and homilies. Hence, in some cases, Du Bois addressed his remarks to "boys and girls" and in other cases to "men and women." It is also to be borne in mind that Du Bois was addressing children or quite young adults who had mostly come from rural or small urban areas, and that most of them were the children or grandchildren of slaves, for emancipation was but forty-five years earlier.

Du Bois's familiarity with Biblical literature is dramatically illustrated in this work; it is reflected also in the entire body of his published writings, manifested in Biblical language, images and themes, especially in his poetry and short stories. Neither in his youth nor in later life did Du Bois attend any church with any regularity, but he was well aware of the enormous influence of the church upon the history and lives of Black people and upon his own life. Two of the fourteen chapters in his immortal *The Souls of Black Folk* (1903) deal directly with this subject—"Of the Faith of the Fathers" and "Of the Sorrow Songs"—and others, such as the essay on Alexander Crummell and the opening chapter, "Of Our Spiritual Strivings," are pervaded by religiosity.

The fact is that Du Bois disliked denominational religion and detested that "Christianity" which became an excuse for the status quo—whether slavery or racism or

---

*Du Bois wrote a fairly detailed history of old Atlanta University in an essay published in *From Servitude to Service: Being the Old South Lectures on the History and Work of Southern Institutions for the Education of the Negro* (Boston: American Unitarian Association, 1905), pp. 155–97. The largely documentary account by a former president, Myron W. Adams, *A History of Atlanta University* (Atlanta University Press, 1930) is helpful; Du Bois briefly reviewed that volume in *The Crisis* 38:16 (January, 1931).

war: the religion, as he once put it, of J. P. Morgan rather than of Jesus Christ. A reason for this sharp feeling was Du Bois's admiration for what he took to be the revolutionary, or at least radical and challenging, character of the actual teachings of Jesus. If Du Bois is not the first who writes of a Black God, he is certainly among the earliest to express this view and he repeatedly draws a parallel between lynching as practiced by Americans and crucifixion as practiced by the Romans.

Du Bois venerated—his word—such Black religious leaders as Bishops Daniel Payne and Benjamin Lee of the African Methodist Church (as evidenced by his column in *Chicago Defender*, January 4, 1947); he viewed the Black church as, at its best, the "basic rock" of his people, their shield and sword, their solace and goad; an indispensable source of their persistence and historical confidence despite all oppression.

John Brown personified Du Bois's ideal of a religious person, and Du Bois admired the Social Christianity of his friends John Haynes Holmes, Willard Uphaus, Stephen Fritchman, Jenkin Lloyd Jones, Francis J. Grimké, George F. Miller, William H. Melish—not to speak of Martin Luther King, Jr.

Personally, too, Du Bois never lost a certain sense of religiosity, of some possible supernatural creative force. In many respects, Du Bois's religious outlook in his last two or three decades might be classified as agnostic, but certainly not atheistic; this remained true even when he chose to join the Communist Party.

The Du Bois of the *Prayers* certainly is not the Du Bois who conducted the Atlanta University Studies during the late nineteenth and early twentieth centuries. The Studies were meant for mature scholars and public-spirited people—Black and white—seeking comprehension of an intricate social question. Nor is this the Du Bois who inspired and led the Niagara Movement for half a decade beginning in 1905. That was a movement of militant Black people, publicly defying the racist policies of the nation and uniting for resistance and struggle against jim crow. Certainly this is not the Du Bois whose anguish produced the immortal *Litany at Atlanta,* after the awful pogrom of 1906. That was written for a leading white liberal weekly of the time in an effort to convey some sense of the horror, near-despair, and seething hatred that Black people felt in the face of the white lynchers. The Du Bois of the *Prayers* is another side of the activist who, at the time of their creation, was engaged in helping to organize the then quite radical National Association for the Advancement of Colored People in which Black and white militants hoped to create a new Abolitionist movement.

These prayers show another facet of the complex totality of Du Bois—a facet rarely seen—which adds to their interest. This is the private and young Du Bois, not in the act of agitating among peers or challenging an ignorant, racist foe. No, this is a Du Bois quietly talking to children and young people, as in a family group, and discussing how to care for oneself, the value of courtesy, the need for excellent work habits, of respect for elders and parents, the importance of inner preparation for the greater tasks, labors, and challenges such not fully mature folk would require with adulthood—especially in a hostile world.

Among the obligations of faith, both Testaments teach, are working hard, taking risks and enduring sacrifice. Du Bois held fast to this outlook throughout his life and in these prayers he was telling his young charges to follow that path. Elevated sermons and uplifting speeches to students are not rare; in Du Bois, however, students saw a preacher and teacher who lived in accordance with what he said.

Indeed, a feature of the sermons that follow is their

autobiographical character. From the time his mother warned him to keep out of saloons, and little Willie had joined a total abstinence society back in Great Barrington in the 1870s, until his death, Du Bois avoided hard liquor. Here he tells his charges to do the same.

Du Bois's promptness was legendary and his sartorial care was extreme; these characteristics also are urged upon his students. Du Bois valued courtesy and saw its pursuit as a hallmark of civilized behavior helping to make life less onerous; this view also appears in these sermons.

Part of courtesy was thoughtfulness—for parents, for elderly people, for the handicapped, for the needy; Du Bois lived that way and called for others to see its value.

Civilized and courteous behavior ruled out racism and male chauvinism, which made peaceful living impossible, and without peace how could there be decent community among peoples?

Du Bois was consciously persistent, dogged; losing was excusable but not trying was sinful. Work was the great purpose; and that work had as its goal human betterment—especially, to begin with, the elevation of one's own people. But love for one's own must not be contaminated by contempt for others.

To suffer in such causes was to be expected; the suffering would not consume, however; rather, it would ennoble.

Du Bois hated waste, and his care with money was great. He kept a careful budget for himself—down to notebook costs when he was a student—and he urged such practices upon his daughter and granddaughter with great seriousness and detail. Du Bois's honesty was fierce; no one dared impugn his integrity and when this was even hinted—as in the case of an implied charge from Robert S. Abbott, founder-owner of the

Chicago Defender—relationship was severed for years until proper apology was forthcoming.

Du Bois's sense of commitment to struggle carried with it confidence in the possibility of achievement; he very early understood, as he notes in one of the sermons, that *"Power* lies buried here" and the italics came from him. Just as the idea of a Black God can be found in Du Bois early in the twentieth century, so the idea of Black Power reappears in his writings and plans during the same period.

The passage from Esther—"I will go unto the King and if I perish, I perish"—that appears in one of these prayers was quoted by Du Bois in his own diary when he was telling himself what he had to do with his life, back in 1893, when he was a student in Berlin. He lived in accordance with that challenge to himself and he is in deadly earnest when he urges the youngsters who heard him to do likewise.

Above all, in his life and in these prayers for dark people, Du Bois believed in work and more work, and in service regardless of cost and sacrifice, to the end of creating a Good Life for all on earth. In this sense, the pages that follow may be read as an autobiographical guide to the beliefs, hopes and practices of W. E. B. Du Bois.

Herbert Aptheker
November 1979

W. E. B. DU BOIS

Prayers for Dark People

Edited by Herbert Aptheker

THE UNIVERSITY OF MASSACHUSETTS PRESS

AMHERST

WAR

POVERTY

ORPHANS

CRIPPLES

SICK

INSANE

TOILERS IN MINES

TUBERCULOSIS

CHILDREN

CHARITY

CRIMINALS

TRADE UNIONS

WOMEN'S SUFFRAGE

OLD AGE

SCIENCE

ART

Help us to remember, O Lord, in this beginning of the year that the man who makes and breaks his New Year's resolves is at least better than the man who makes none. Deliver us from such sloth and self-satisfaction as see no evil and recognize no possible improvement or are too lazy to attempt the good. Give us courage to fail in a good cause, and determination never to cease striving toward that which God, His world and our own hearts tell us is worthwhile. *Wherefore, O Lord, shall the world count its steps from that dark cross on Calvary, if those steps be not really toil and slipping and back-sliding and yet withal that forward-coming toward Thee. Amen.*

EXODUS 12:1–3, 11–14

Defend, O Lord, this Thy land from the curse of drunkenness. Guide aright the oft misguided enthusiasm of those, beneath whose striving lies the terrible truth of our national weakness. Let the life of him who was born 100 years ago this night* live as both warning and inspiration to the young—the beauty of his song, the wonder of his genius, the shame of his slavery to drink. We are glad of his life even though he sinned, but we tremble at the strength of his and our weakness, O God, and pray for Thy strength. Amen.

ISAIAH 28:1–4,7

---

*It appears likely the reference is to Edgar Allen Poe, born January 19, 1809.

4

Give us this night, O God, Peace in our land and the long silence that comes after strain and up-heaval. Let us sense the solemnity of this day—its mighty meaning, its deep duty. Save this government. Cherish its great ideals—give strength and honesty and unbending courage to him whom the people today have named Chief Magistrate of these United States and make our country in truth a land where all men are free and equal in the pursuit of happiness. Amen.

Lord of the springtime, Father of flower, field and fruit, smile on us in these earnest days when the work is heavy and the toil wearisome; lift up our hearts, O God, to the things worthwhile—sunshine and night, the dripping rain, the song of the birds, books and music, and the voices of our friends. Lift up our hearts to these this night, O Father, and grant us Thy peace. Amen.

REVELATIONS 21:1–4

The earth about us, O Lord, is swelling
with fruitage and may it remind us that this is the seed
time of life. That not today, not tomorrow, will come
the true reaping of the deeds we do now, but in some far,
veiled and mighty harvest. Let us then learn to treat
this, which is the springtime to so many of us, with
reverence and thoughtfulness, not deceiving ourselves
with the apparent ease of Evil now, but looking toward
the harvest when the earth shall be not ours but the
Lord's, and the fullness thereof.

MICAH 6:1–4,15–16

Keep us, O Lord, from the fallacy of thinking that it is only the whole of a deed that can be well done. A bad deed well-ended is better than a deed wholly bad. A school year whose December had been thrown away may be *in part* retrieved in May. The neglected education of a child may be saved from ignorance in youth. It is *never* too late to mend. Nothing is so bad that good may not be put into it and make it better and save it from utter loss. Strengthen in us this knowledge and faith and hope, O God, in these last days. Amen.

Now, O Lord, Thy world begins—this is Commencement, the day when these our brothers and sisters step forward into Life, and the realness of Things, and we whom they leave behind lift hand and heart in greeting. God speed the way of these whose* stand on the mighty threshold of the elect of those chosen souls born and bred into the common wealth of knowledge and the kingdoms of culture. And so tonight we wave our greetings to our fellows and bless with that blessing of the ages: the Lord bless you and keep you, the Lord make His face to shine upon you and be gracious with you—the Lord lift up the Light of His countenance upon you and give you War[‡] that out of the dust of battle and travail of soul, bitterness of defeat and anguish of sorrow, some day shall come forth the Perfect Soul.

---

*So in the original, meaning "who."
‡The word *peace* was crossed out by Du Bois and *War* put in its place.

O God, teach us who are looking eagerly forward to the great play-time of the year to weigh wisely and well the seriousness of play. How many men have worked well in their work-time and then destroyed soul and body in their mistaken play. How many women have found their glory in work and their perdition in mistaken rest. We would learn, Our Father, to choose our recreations as thoughtfully as our duties—to bring them in and mingle them with our work—to make our life a oneness of work and rest-in-work, of rest and work-in-rest and of Joy in both and not a contradiction of life-building and waste of energy and debauchery, right and wrong. Amen.

ECCLESIASTES 2:4–11

Long days we have sighed for liberty and lo! Thy Freedom, O Lord, is at our doors. We welcome it even as we welcome life: the careless see idleness and emptiness—the thoughtful see the vigorous delight of turning to new scenes, new duties and new responsibilities. Herein we test the strength, the steadfastness, the depth of our training: if summer freedom means to us license and selfishness and irregularity, then we are not free but prisoned still in ignorance. But if vacation shall mean renewed service to Goodness and Beauty then we enter the higher broader rest, where Thy truth shall make us free. Amen.

HEBREWS 12:1–6

Give us thankful hearts, O God, in this the season of Thy Thanksgiving. May we be thankful for health and strength, for sun and rain and peace. Let us seize the day and the opportunity and strive for that greatness of spirit that measures life not by its disappointments but by its possibilities, and let us ever remember that true gratitude and appreciation shows itself neither in independence nor satisfaction but passes the gift joyfully on in larger and better form. Such gratitude grant us, O Lord. Amen.

PSALM 100

Teach us, O God, in this season of approaching holiday that we who are so used to receiving the bounty of others are missing the most of life, if we do not learn the Joy of giving. We make our friends happier by giving, and happy friends are themselves the best of God's gifts. We make the world better by the gift of our service and our selves, and it is a better world that we ourselves need. So in some mystic way does God bring realization through sacrifice and this is the greatest lesson youth may learn. Amen.

ACTS 20:31–36

Protect us, O God, as the season of Thy festival draws near. Give us the spirit of Peace and Joy and good-will toward men. Send us to our homes with tidings of good cheer or send the spirit of home to us here with all its warmth and blessing. Let *our* rest be without dissipation, *our* Joy without noise, and from the riot and drunkenness about us, protect us, O Lord. Amen.

MARK 1:1–7

In the solemn silence of this Thy Holy night, O Heavenly Father, let the Christ spirit be born anew in this our home and in this land of ours. Out of the depths of selfishness and languor and envy, let spring the spirit of humility and poverty, of gentleness and sacrifice—the eternal dawn of Peace, good-will toward men. Let the birth-bells of God call our vain imaginings back from pomp and glory and wealth— back from the wasteful warships searching the seas— back to the lowly barn-yard and the homely cradle of a yellow and despised Jew, whom the world has not yet learned to call Wonderful, Counsellor, the Mighty God, the Everlasting Father, and the Prince of Peace. Amen.

We pray tonight, O God, for confidence in ourselves, our powers and our purposes in this beginning of a New Year. Ward us from all lack of faith and hesitancy and inspire in us not only the determination to do a year's work well, but the unfaltering belief that what we wish to do, we will do. Such Faith, O Lord, is born of Works. Every deed accomplished finishes not only itself but is fallow ground for future deeds. Abundantly endow us, Our Father, with this deed-born Faith. Amen.

JAMES 2:14–24

In Thy words, O Father: He that shall endure to the end shall be praised: these are the natural days for listlessness and a shirking—for looking backward when our hands are yet to the plow—for wishing rest before rest is earned. Give us persistence and endurance, O God, in these days of ending; give us to remember the ceaseless plodding and the unwearying exercise of hand and brain are the things that bring real strength and knowledge. Is not the end of a thing greater than the beginning and shall not our work at the year's close be finer and truer and better than at its wavering beginnings? Amen.

ECCLESIASTES 12:1–4

In these first beginnings of the new life of the world, renew in us the resolution to persist in the good work we have begun. Give us strength of body and strength of mind and the unfaltering determination to carry out that which we know to be good and right. Forgive all wavering in the past service of Thy cause and make us strong to go forward in spite of the doubts of our friends and our enemies and in spite of our own distrust in ourselves. Out of the death of winter comes ever and again the resurrection of spring: so out of evil bring good, O God, and out of doubt determination. Amen.

JOHN 2:17–25

May the Lord give us both the honesty and strength to look our own faults squarely in the face and not ever continue to excuse and minimize them, while they grow. Grant us that wide view of ourselves which our neighbors possess, or better the highest view of infinite justice and goodness and efficiency. In that great white light let us see the littleness and narrowness of our souls and the deeds of our days, and then forthwith begin their betterment. Only thus shall we broaden out of the vicious circle of our own admiration into the greater commendation of God. Amen.*

PSALM 80

---

*On the reverse of the sheet of paper upon which this was written appears, in Du Bois's hand: "May 3, 1910."

Help us to hope that the seeming Shadow of this Death is to our human blindness but the exceeding brightness of a newer greater life.

Give us grace, O God, to dare to do the deed which we well know cries to be done. Let us not hesitate because of ease, or the words of men's mouths, or our own lives. Mighty causes are calling us—the freeing of women, the training of children, the putting down of hate and murder and poverty—all these and more. But they call with voices that mean work and sacrifice and death. Mercifully grant us, O God, the spirit of Esther, that we say: I will go unto the King and if I perish, I perish—Amen.

ESTHER 4:9–16

Remember, O God, thru'out the world this night those who struggle for better government and freer institutions. Help us to realize that our brothers are not simply those of our own blood and nation, but far more are they those who think as we do and strive toward the same ideals. So tonight in Persia and China, in Russia and Turkey, in Africa and all America, let us bow with our brothers and sisters and pray as they pray for a world, well-governed—void of war and caste, and free to each asking soul. Amen.

I SAMUEL 13:11–14

Strengthen in us each tonight, O Lord, that silence* sense of Honor—the Honor of our Home, the Honor of our School, the Honor of our Race and the Honor of Thy name. Let us ever see more and more clearly the deed which in the face of our own self-respect we dare not stoop to do. Let us recognize the glory of sacrifice for the good name of those souls we love and those things we revere. And let us value achievement not for what it brings to us but rather for what it gives to a starving struggling world. Amen.

GENESIS 27:18–24

---

*Thus in the original; apparently, "silent" was meant.

Give us, O God, the gift of human charity. Lead us to know that bad as human nature is and black as our passion may be, that most men are always a little better than the worst, always more decent than our rash judgment tries to paint. Give us the humility to realize that few of us put in their places—with their hurts and hindrances and their vision of right—few of us would do better than they, and many would do far worse. Perhaps God meant just this when He said: *Blessed* are the meek. Amen.

ST. LUKE 6:27–36

We thank Thee, O Lord, for the gift of Death
—for the great silence that follows the jarring noises of
the world—the rest that is Peace. We who live to see the
passing of that fine and simple Old Man, who has so
often sat beside us here in this room, must not forget the
legacy he leaves us or the Hope he still holds to us: we
are richer for his sacrifice, truer for his honesty and
better for his goodness. And his living leaves us firm
in the faith that the Kingdom of Heaven will yet reign
among men.

Help us, O Lord, to remember our kindred beyond the sea—all those who bend in bonds, of our own blood and of human kind—the lowly and the wretched, the ignorant and the weak. We are one world, O God, and one great human problem and what we do here goes to solve not our petty troubles alone but the difficulties and desires of millions unborn and unknown. Let us then realize our responsibilities and gain strength to bear them worthily—Amen.

PSALM 46

In the midst of life and deeds it is easy to have endurance and strength and determination, but Thy Word, O Lord, teaches us, that this is not enough to bring good to the world—to bring happiness and the worthier success. For *this* we must endure to the end—learn to finish things—to bring them to accomplishment and full fruition. We must not be content with plans, ambitions and resolves; with part of a message or part of an education, but be set and determined to fulfill the promise and complete the task and secure the full training. Such men and women alone does God save by lifting them above and raising them to higher worlds and wider prospects. Give us then, O God, to resist today the temptation of shirking, and the grit to endure to the end. Amen.

MATTHEW 24:6–13

God give us grace to realize that education is not simply *doing* the things we like, *studying* the tasks that appeal to us, or wandering in the world of thought *whither* and *where* we will. In a universe where *good* is hidden underneath *evil* and *pleasure* lurks in *pain*, we must work if we would *learn* and *know*. It is the *unpleasant* task, the *hard* lesson, the *bitter* experience that often leads to knowledge and power and good. Let us, O Lord, learn this in the days of youth while the evil days come not, nor the years draw nigh, when Thou shalt say, "I have no pleasure in them."

ECCLESIASTES 11: 1–7

Grant us, O God, the vision and the will to be found on the right side in the great battle for bread, which rages round us, in strike and turmoil and litigation. Let us remember that here as so often elsewhere no impossible wisdom is asked of men, only Thine ancient sacrifice—to do justly and love mercy and walk humbly—to refuse to use, of the world's goods, more than we earn, to be generous with those that earn but little and to avoid the vulgarity that flaunts wealth and clothes and ribbons in the face of poverty. These things are the sins that lie beneath our labor wars, and from such sins defend us, O Lord. Amen.

MICAH 6: 1–8

Defend, O Lord, these Thy children in all their work and all their play. Spread among them the desire to know and learn and do. Let them grow in the capacity for worthy work and in all their working and thinking let them not forget the host of witnesses about them—those that love and those that inspire—and may they in the end prove worthy of their great heritage. Amen.

The Lord make us mindful of the little things that grow and blossom in these days to make the world beautiful for us. Teach us to reverence in this world not simply the great and impressive but all the minute and myriad-sided beauty of field and flower and tree. And as we worship these, so in our lives let us strive not for the masterful and spectacular but for the good and true, not for the thunder but for the still small voice of duty. Amen.

O Thou light of the world, shine in upon our darkness and illumine the truth that all men may see it. For men are more ignorant than wicked—willfully ignorant it is true and wickedly willful—and yet it is because the world does not know and realize the truth about itself and about its human children that it is continually doing such monstrous and hurtful things. Give us then light, more light, O God, that we may see and learn and know and we may no longer be with them that sit in darkness.

JOHN 8:12–16

Let us remember, O God, that our religion in life is expressed in our work, and therefore in this school it is shown in the way we conquer our studies—not entirely in our marks but in the honesty of our endeavor, the thoroughness of our accomplishment and the singleness and purity of our purpose. In school life there is but one unforgivable sin and that is to know how to study and to be able to study, and then to waste and throw away God's time and opportunity. From this blasphemy deliver us all, O God. Amen.

God grant us the desire to be useful—to look upon ourselves not simply as centers of pleasure and good, but rather as instruments in Thy hands for helping and cheering and doing. We would not forget, O God, that great and wonderful as this Thy world is, it holds but dross and disappointment for them that seek simply to enjoy it. Only to those who seek life in the happiness of human souls, and in the service of those whom Thou hast builded in Thine own image—only then and to them are the secret treasures of the world revealed. This is the lesson of life. May we learn it. Amen.

PSALM 119:9–16

We ask Thee tonight, O God, for better government in this land; for a keener sense of responsibility among those in authority—remembering that public office is not for private gain but for the greater good of all. Give to those who choose officials equal realization of the great responsibility that rests on them, knowing that a land is after all what its voters make it. Let us realize too that even we the disfranchised have our duties—the duty of thorough preparation, the duty of careful observation, the duty of intelligent criticism. All these things go to make a civilized Christian state, such as we wish our land to be. Amen.

I SAMUEL 8:10–19

Teach us, O God, that NOW is the accepted time—not tomorrow, not some more convenient season. It is *today* that our best studying can be done and not some future day or future year. It is *today* that we fit ourselves for the greater usefulness of tomorrow. *Today* is the seed time, *now* are the hours of work and tomorrow comes the harvest and the play-time. May we learn in youth, when the evil days come not, that the man who plays and then works, rests and then studies, fails and then rushes, is not simply reversing nature, he is missing opportunities and losing the training and preparation which makes work and study and endeavor the touchstone of success.

ISAIAH 49:8–11

We pray, O Lord, tonight for the cause of education in this land. Open Thou the door of opportunity to little children of every race and condition and let them know the world they live in and its possibilities. Inspire those in authority to deal largely and abundantly with the public funds that support instruction. Teach parents to strive and sacrifice, that their children may not grow up in ignorance and sin because of darkness, and finally inspire in us some appreciation of the vast meaning and infinite good of a school like this. Amen.

LUKE 2:40–49

God bless the wanderers—they that seek and seldom find and yet all ceaselessly do seek some Truer, Better Thing—some fairer country. These are they, O Lord, who open up the hidden ways of earth and men: for the way of the wanderer is wide and winding, his soul hungers after God—always are his paths weary and without end. Yet we feel his kinship to us all, we glory in his findings, we enter into his heritage. God save his soul tonight wherever he may be and give our yearning following spirits Peace. Amen.

O God, teach us to know that failure is as much a part of life as success—and whether it shall be evil or good depends upon the way we meet it—if we face it listlessly and daunted, angrily or vengefully, then indeed is it evil for it spells death. But if we let our failures stand as guideposts and as warnings—as beacons and as guardians—then is honest failure far better than stolen success, and but a part of that great training which God gives us to make us women and men. The race is not to the swift—nor the battle to the strong, O God. Amen.

Give us Grace, O God, to remember Thy great commandment: Thou shalt not steal. This nation in its greed and haste is like to become a den of thieves and we, who half-consciously follow the spirit of our surrounding, are not careful enough of that which is not ours. May we in youth learn to reverence not only the *Things* that belong to our neighbors, but the Thoughts and the Time, the Rights and the good Name of all our fellows which lie so largely in our keeping; make us jealous, O God, to protect and care for our neighbors' property even as our own; make us thoughtful to care for the property of this institution, lest we steal from the widow and the orphan, and finally make us careful of our own selves lest we steal from Thee, O God. Amen.

LEVITICUS 19:11–16

Remember with us tonight, O God, our kindred beyond the seas; they that sit in darkness without the shining of the mighty light that beats upon these leading lands. Forget them not, O God, for they are Thine and ours. Human in all their weakness and built in love and joy and sorrow, even as we. Hasten the day when the barriers shall fall and the heathen shall be blood brothers to us all in deed as well as word. That this is the greatest work lying to our hands, teach us, O God.

ISAIAH 43

God give us the grace to remember that some failures are our own fault and ours alone. Envy and unkindness, prejudice and hardness of heart may do much to keep men back in the world and drag them down. But when all that is said and done, teach us, O God, to know that our own laziness and carelessness and sin are the heaviest weights about our feet. To escape from all these in true repentance and lofty resolve give Thy Help, O God. Amen.

I SAMUEL 15

It is the wind and the rain, O God, the cold and the storm that make this earth of Thine to blossom and bear its fruit. So in our lives it is storm and stress and hurt and suffering that make real men and women bring the world's work to its highest perfection. Let us learn then in these growing years to respect the harder sterner aspects of life together with its joy and laughter, and to weave them all into the great web which hangs holy to the Lord—Amen.

JOEL 2:21–7

Therefore also we pray always for you that our God would count *you* worthy of this calling and *fulfill* all the good pleasures of *His* goodness, and the work of *faith,* with *power.*

Let us not forget, O Lord, that the real world is a world of sunshine and flowers; that across this sweeter truer life flit all too often the shadows of sin and sorrow and death—the unreality of silent and sad winter. But let us not, O Father, deceive ourselves herewith—let us not fail to recognize and welcome in fullness of Joy the spring when it comes, the Truth when it blossoms. Behind all error and wrong and injustice may we ever scent the far-off subtle fragrance of everlasting flowers. Amen.

Remember with us tonight, O God, the old and helpless—those who have reached length of days and known life with its joys and bitterness and have come in the evening to the long shadows, unloved and uncared for and alone. May we in our youth and gladness and plenty never forget these silent sentinels of pain and neglect who stand to warn us against extravagance and undutifulness and careless ease. Someone has forgotten his duty toward each of these pitiful souls. May we never forget our duty which Thy voice sounded from Sinai: Honor thy father and thy mother that their days may be long in the Land—Amen.

GENESIS 48

Our Father, we acknowledge our manifold sins—we do earnestly repent and are heartily sorry for these our misdoings. We have done those things we ought not to have done and we have left undone those things we ought to have done. Have mercy upon us, O God, and teach us to have mercy on ourselves by learning never to follow a first mistake by a second— always to learn the future by the past, and ever to rise on stepping stones of our dead selves to higher things. Amen.

PSALM 120

Remember with us tonight, O God, the homes that own us all. Make us true to the fathers and mothers of these children here—true to their hopes and ideals, careful of their hard-earned money, appreciative of their love and care. On the strength of the home hang many things—the training of children in a far deeper sense than we can train them here; the saving of wealth; and above all the fulfillment of the great word which Thou hast spoken—Honor thy father and thy mother, that thy days may be long upon the land which the Lord Thy God giveth thee. Remember with us tonight, O God, the fathers and mothers of these children here and the homes they have left. Give them grace to realize the vast significance of the family group in their lives and let us all know that here we but build on foundations laid there and we build best on homes where truth is taught and reverence and where Thy word is heard. Honor thy father and thy mother that their days may be long upon the land which the Lord Thy God giveth thee.

GENESIS 22

Let us remember tonight those who are in the bonds of poverty who have neither sufficient food nor drink, the beauty of home or the love of beauty. Bring us the day, O God, when the world shall no longer know such poverty as stunts growth and feeds crime, and teach us to realize that such things are not necessary to earth but are the result of our greed and selfishness, our wastefulness and willful forgetting. Amen.

LUKE 16:19

May God deliver us from the curse of carelessness, from the thoughtless ill-considered deed. The deliberate evil of the world, we know is great, but how much of fortitude and strength and faith could we have to cure this and put it down, if only we were rid of the sickening discouraging mass of thoughtless careless acts in men who know and mean better. How willingly in all these years and now, have thousands of mothers and fathers toiled and sweat and watched from dawn till midnight over these children here, only to be rewarded—not indeed by crime, but by persistent carelessness almost worse than crime. The rules here are the simple rules of work and growth. We do not make them—the very circumstances of our life make them. And when we break them, it is *not* because we reason *out* their *un*reasonableness but usually because we do not think—because back of Law and Order we are too lazy to see the weary pain-scarred heart of the mother who sent us here. God give us vision and thought. Amen.

This is the day, O God, when the floods of Thy World-Sunshine billow over our lives, and the shimmer and shine of things make it seem good and pleasant to walk on green earth. Let us enjoy all that Thou, Father, hast given us—but let us do more than enjoy; let us work while day dawns and sow for the Harvest and strive for that Inner Light, which shall shine in the day when suns fail and moons are dim and the Joy of living seems trembling to the dust. Give us this wisdom in this Thy day, O God, and in Thy night, rest. Amen.

ECCLESIASTES 11:6–9, 12:1–7

O Lord, teach us who love Liberty and long for it, to realize its cost and purpose. There can be no freedom in a just and good world, if freedom means to do as we please, when we please, and where all about us in this life, as in this school, lie bars and bonds and limits. The free are those who know the rules which God Himself has set and go their way within these metes and bounds full freely. Truth is the knowledge of these strait and narrow ways. It is the Truth that makes us free and this it is we linger here to learn, O Lord. Amen.

JOHN 8:31–36

God bless all schools and forward the great work of education for which we stand. Arouse within us and within our land a deep realization of the seriousness of our problem of training children. On them rests the future work and thought and sentiment and goodness of the world. If here and elsewhere we train the lazy and shallow, the self-indulgent and the frivolous—if we destroy reason and religion and do not rebuild, help us, O God, to realize how heavy is our responsibility and how great the cost. The school of today is the world of tomorrow and today and tomorrow are Thine, O God. Amen.

I SAMUEL 16:6–12

Forget not, O God, those who are crippled and maimed in body, who have not the free use of hand and limb as we have; who cannot walk in the fresh clear air or know the Joy of action, motion and bounding blood. May we not forget this mighty blessing of physical strength and straightness. May we not foolishly mar or spoil our bodies, but make them ever fair and fairer temples for the indwelling of Thine own spirit, O God. Amen.

JOB 6:1–4, 11–14

54

As the season when the home with parents and children and friends becomes the center of so much that is beautiful and good, let us not, O God, forget them that are homeless and friendless—who see and know but little of the world beautiful, but bend only beneath its ugliness and drudgery and sin. Let us not forget them, O God, lay their sorrows on our hearts as some slight atonement for our sin and let the good-will thou sendest to earth be not simply for the good and well-cared for, but for all men through our own deeds and kindliness. Amen.

MATTHEW 25:34–40

Teach us, O God, that *pride* in our school, our race and our generation that brings with it no unworthy wish for other schools and other peoples and other days. The self and individuality of men and nations are mighty things wherewith God plans to make the earth broader and richer and which we must cherish and develop so schools and homes have their own hardwon ideals and ways: make us, O God, true to ourselves, to the race that needs us and to this school which is and may be so vast an instrument of good. But whatever we strive to be and do, let it mean but appreciation and good-will toward the striving of others. Amen.

LUKE 15:21–28

Once they tell us, Jehovah, that in the great shadows of the past Thou hast whispered to a quivering people, saying, "Be not afraid." He watching over Israel slumbers not nor sleeps. Grant us today, O God, that fearlessness that rests on confidence in the ultimate rightness of things. Let us be afraid neither of mere physical hurt, nor of the unfashionableness of our color, nor of the unpopularity of our cause; let us turn toward the battle of life undismayed and above all when we have fought the good fight grant us to face the shadow of death with the same courage that has let us live. Amen.

PSALM 121

G ive us in our day, O God, to see the fulfillment of Thy vision of Peace. May these young people grow to despise false ideals of conquest and empire and all the tinsel of war. May we strive to replace force with justice and armies of murder with armies of relief. May we believe in Peace among all nations as a present practical creed and count love for our country as love and not hate for our fellow men. Amen.

MICAH 4: 1–4

God pity them that suffer with hunger and with cold—they to whom the world is but dull and leaden toil, whose pleasures are faded memories or unreal tales of things they know not. God pity them and pity us too, if we have no sympathy for them—if we are not willing here in these halls to dedicate our lives to the lessening of their sorrow, and the uprooting of their poverty and to the broadening of life and living for all human souls. Amen.

MATTHEW 25:34–40

There is no God but Love and Work is His prophet—help us to realize this truth, O Father, which Thou so often in word and deed has taught us. Let the knowledge temper our ambitions and our judgments. We would not be great but busy—not pious but sympathetic—not merely reverent, but filled with the glory of our Life-Work. God is Love and Work is His Revelation. Amen.

JOHN 4:7–12

We thank thee, O God, for the gift of death, for the great silence that comes after the noise and strife of this world. Yet we ask, if a man die shall he live again? To this cry of ages, O Heavenly Father, Easter has answered again, that great festival to immortality. The earth was dead and lo! it lives again; the grass is struggling beneath our thoughtless feet, the flowers we wantonly pick and waste are blooming; the Christ was crucified and lo his spirit still strives with men. The valley of the shadow of death is dark and all of us here, young and old and bad and good, must yet face silent and alone. Beyond, the How and What and Where of those many mansions, Thou hast not said, O God, but this we know: we shall in some wise live—not surely in body, in soul we trust, and certainly in the deeds we do now, the memories we leave, the lives we influence and the ideals in which we dream. Of such and all immortal life make us worthy, O God—Amen.

REVELATION 22:10–17

Immortality

God teach us to work. Herein alone do we approach our Creator when we stretch our arms with toil, and strain with eye and ear and brain to catch the thought and do the deed and create the things that make life worth living. Let us quickly learn in our youth, O Father, that in the very doing, the honest humble determined striving, lies the realness of things, the great glory of life. Of all things there is fear and fading— beauty pales and hope disappoints; but blessed is the worker—his are the kingdoms of earth—Amen.

JAMES 2:4–17
PSALM 67

Work

2

O Thou Incarnate Word of God to man,
make us this Christmas night to realize Thy truth: we
are not Christians because we profess Thy name and
celebrate the ceremonies and idly reiterate the prayers
of the church, but only in so far as we really compre-
hend and follow the Christ spirit—we must be poor and
not rich, meek and not proud, merciful and not oppres-
sors, peaceful and not warlike or quarrelsome. For the
sake of the righteousness of our cause we must bow to
persecution and reviling, and again and again turn the
stricken cheek to the striker; and above all the cause of
our neighbor must be to us dearer than our own cause.
This is Christianity. God help us all to be Christians.
Amen.

LUKE 2:8–14

Christmas

3

O God, these are the days when Thou spreadest before us the wide sweet cleanness of a great New Year. To us this will be a year of no ordinary happenings but heavy with deeds. Some of us *it* will turn toward strength and determination, and good deeds, and some toward weakness and hesitation and deeds of shame. And lest we be the ones who fall and offend, let us all here, teacher and student, boy and girl, bow and pray that the coming year shall give us courage tempered with courtesy; make us good and yet strong, cheerful but not boisterous, persistent and self-controlled, ambitious but unselfish, grateful and yet independent, humble but not slavish, reverent but not superstitious, and ever and always patient. Give us faith in ourselves, hope for our cause and love for our fellows—faith, hope and love, these three and the greatest of these is love. Amen.

EXODUS 12:1–3,7,11–15

New Year

4

Tonight, O Father, in the beginning of this week of praying, we ask especially for reverence. These are the days and this is rightly the place of criticism and searching—of the insistent questionings of old beliefs and old ways and old deeds; of quick recognition of error and superstition. But Thou, O God, whom our fathers called the ancient of days, make it also a place for joyfully recognizing and reverently welcoming the things that are good and true and the eternal beauty of both new and old. Make us ever mindful of the solemnness of world-old things, of the rightness of the old homely ways. Make us ever reverent toward truth, whether new or old, make us ever respectful toward right, whether ragged or laced; and above all, in these the days of our eager knowing, give us pause to listen to the still small voice that whispers within us always, till* we deafen our souls to its pleading. Amen.

PSALM 68:28–35

Reverence

---

*Thus in the original; apparently Du Bois meant "lest" not "till."

5

Our Heavenly Father, teach us this night
and ever to remember that Thou hatest a lie, for a
lie is a pitiable, degrading and dangerous thing. Dangerous to a universe whose foundations are God's
Truth, degrading to young growing characters which
should be open, honest and sincere; and pitiable for
boys and girls like these who ought to despise deception
and deceit. Create in us, O God, that high sense of honor
and self-respect which will suffer disgrace and punish-
ment rather than stoop to a falsehood. [Well we know,
our Father, that among us here, it is not so much the
great deceptions as it is the little lies, the petty fibbing
that hurts—things too small for the world's true
workers to soil their souls with.] Deliver us from tat-
tlers, tale-bearers and liars. Teach us that silence may
save us from such things but that a lie can never save
a human soul from* its own damnation and the world's
disgust. [We live in the midst of lies, O God. Slavery was
a lie and much of this problem of races is a mass of lies.

*In the original after the word "from" appears "aught but"; these words have
been stricken above since they contradict Du Bois's manifest meaning.
Note: Bracketed sentences were encircled in pencil in the original, as though
they were meant to be omitted, but this is not certain.

But may we as Christians and as men rise above our surroundings and become true and honest men and women, abhorring whatsoever worketh abomination or maketh a lie.] Amen.

ACTS 5:1–6

Lies

6

God give us courtesy—give us pause in the rush and whirl of life for the little kindnesses and gentle manners that make the wide difference between life and death-in-life. May we never forget that true dignity and self-respect do not fear for themselves, but ever prefer the calm quiet of conscious power to the boisterousness of pretension. They do not ask, they give. It does not hurt the noble-born to bow unbidden, to plead unanswered or to be silent under scorn. Tonight, tomorrow and henceforward, we, both teacher and taught, would be with them that walk in courtesy and the shadow of Thy mighty love. Amen.

LUKE 10:30–35
PETER 3:8–12

Courtesy

7

We pray tonight for strength—for strength of body and strength of mind, for strength of soul and strength of faith. Help us, Our Father, to realize how far we ourselves are responsible for weakness, sickness and death; help us to know that success in study is far more a matter of work than of gift; above all we would not forget that strength of character like strength of limb comes from constant unwearying exercise. And finally, in the dying of the day, as we go to room and bed, full of strong simple faith that Thy sun will bring tomorrow's light, so strengthen too, in us, this night, *faith* that some fair morning *all* we count good and beautiful will come true. Amen.

JUDGES 15:11–15
PSALMS 18 and 93

Strength

8

The difference between man and beast is this, that Thou, O God, hast planted in us aspiration, ambition, outstretchings toward the dim and far possible, the unresting desire to be more than what we are and truer and better. Bless to us this mighty passion, our Father, and make it a true inspiration and not a selfish temptation. May we realize how wonderful a thing it is to be a healthy human being here on the threshold of a great new century—to taste the heritage of a mighty past, to pile the endowment of a greater future and above all to realize in our own souls all that God meant us to be. Amen.

ISAIAH 52:1–9

Ambition

9

The prayer of our souls this night is a petition for persistence; not for the one good deed, or single thought, but deed on deed, and thought on thought, until day calling unto day shall make a life worth living. We want these young people to grow the grim grit of men who never know they're beaten, never own defeat, but snatch success and victory out of the teeth of failure by keeping everlastingly at work and never giving up. Give us, O God, to walk with him who "never faltered but marched breast forward, never dreamed tho right were vanquished, wrong would triumph, held we fall to rise, and baffled to fight better—sleep to wake."* Amen.

GENESIS 32:24–32

Persistence

---

*This is quoted, not quite accurately, from Robert Browning's *Asolando*— Epilogue, stanza 3:
One who never turned his back but marched breast forward,
  Never doubted clouds would break,
Never dreamed, though right were worsted, wrong would triumph,
  Held we fall to rise, are baffled to fight better,
    Sleep to wake.
Inexact quotation was very common with Du Bois.

10 [Promptness]

God make us prompt to do Thy work.
Sharpen in us the sense of shame at being late at our
Father's business. This is a late land and a tardy
people—the stiffening paralysis of a crawling creeping
past hangs drowsily on our spirit. The spell of the lotus
eaters is upon us; unbind us, God—from the loitering
laziness of everlasting lateness, good Lord, deliver us;
from the hesitancy of lingering and loafing, spare us,
good Lord. We are groping for *light, movement,
strength, decision, deeds*! *Power* lies buried here,
speak then, Father, to these children of Israel that they
go forward to a *prompt* world—a world where never the
sun in all his thousand thousands of years forgets a
second, where never moon loiters to lateness nor yet
a single little star comes straggling tardily across the
sky. Rouse us, quicken us, give us to know that promptness and efficiency lie in the *starting*—that no rush and
sweat can retrieve this initial falseness—that for the
tardy soul there is neither salvation nor success, but *late*
in youth, he is *late* in age, *laggard* in *this* world

with work never begun, in the *next* he shall stand before his Maker—late! Amen.

MATTHEW 25:1–10

Cleanliness

I will be *clean.*

I will be *clean* in *body:* bathing regularly, wearing clean rather than costly clothes, careful of my linen, attentive to my hands and feet, my teeth and my hair, my nose and my ears, especially avoiding unpleasant odors like perspiration and bad breath.

I will be *clean* in *thought,* clean-cut in my reasoning, honest in my allusions, frank in my statements and pure in my imaginings.

I will be *clean* in *soul.* I will not sin knowingly or repeatedly, nor even through ignorance where knowledge is possible.

I will not *steal.*

I will not use used postage stamps, pass bad money, keep lost articles when the loser can be found, borrow without asking, misuse public property.

Teach us, O Lord, to know the value of money. So many of us are spending what we do not earn, that we grow thoughtless and prodigal with the thing that comes to us cheaply, but which represents *so often* the sweat and toil of self-denial of those who love us. How many a boy and girl here tonight is begging the very blood from some mother's heart for the sake of a useless dress or a gaudy necktie or is wasting hard-earned plenty to dazzle the thoughtless and weak. Time is money and money is work and work is Life and he who wastes money wastes the Life that Thou hast given him and his, O God. Amen.

PROVERBS 13:4,7–8,11,18,22–23

Library of Congress Cataloging in Publication Data
Du Bois, William Edward Burghardt, 1868–1963.
Prayers for dark people.

1. Prayers.   2. Afro-American students—Prayer-
books and devotions—English.   3. Pastoral prayers.
I. Aptheker, Herbert, 1915–   II. Title.
BV245.D8 1980   242'.8   80–12234
ISBN 0–87023–303–3 (pbk.)